# Imprints on My Soul

## Poetry In Search of the Beloved

Saira Sabzaali

**BALBOA.**
PRESS

A DIVISION OF HAY HOUSE

ISBN: 978-1-4525-4105-1 (sc)
ISBN: 978-1-4525-4106-8 (e)
Library of Congress Control Number: 2011918355

Balboa Press books may be ordered through booksellers or by contacting:

Balboa Press
A Division of Hay House
1663 Liberty Drive
Bloomington, IN 47403
www.balboapress.com
1-(877) 407-4847

Because of the dynamic nature of the Internet, any web addresses or links contained in this book may have changed since publication and may no longer be valid. The views expressed in this work are solely those of the author and do not necessarily reflect the views of the publisher, and the publisher hereby disclaims any responsibility for them.

The author of this book does not dispense medical advice or prescribe the use of any technique as a form of treatment for physical, emotional, or medical problems without the advice of a physician, either directly or indirectly. The intent of the author is only to offer information of a general nature to help you in your quest for emotional and spiritual well-being. In the event you use any of the information in this book for yourself, which is your constitutional right, the author and the publisher assume no responsibility for your actions.

Any people depicted in stock imagery provided by Thinkstock are models, and such images are being used for illustrative purposes only.
Certain stock imagery © Thinkstock.

Cover art by Saima Jamal.

Printed in the United States of America
Balboa Press rev. date: 11/29/2011

I dedicate this book to my Saheb-ji.

Thank you for your direction, your love, and unwavering faith in me, in all of us. You are my path and my signpost, the air around me and the ground upon which I stand.

I choose only You, in this life and the next.

# Author's Note

Poetry speaks in a way that other literature cannot. When we try to capture the deepest parts of ourselves, or of life, poetry is as close as we can get.

I wrote these poems at a time of falling in love with a man, with an idea, and with my God. I have been immersed in great works of poetry since my childhood, and have taken inspiration from legendary poets and singers from mystical and oral traditions around the world. The poems are a window into my own heart, and I hope they will speak to you in that gentle and powerful language of love, devotion, and change.

# Bowing to the Master

I've been dancing around the frayed edges
Of the Truth
And now He has plunged me into the center

They told me Life was a dialogue
A heated midnight whisper
Between the dancer and her music
Between the poet and his muse

The words jumble when we reach this place
Of familiar strangeness
Of acid paper and smeared ink

The light pours through my fingertips
Opening your heart

Do you feel the shifting?
Do you feel your new self?
The servant bows to the Master

# My First Poem for Him

I spoke to Him once in poetry
The words forming a song that moved us

And when He heard me singing
He laughed

He had been waiting for us to recognize His light
In each other

But we were too busy

Too busy planning and re-planning
Riding to the tops of our ladders

Too busy to remember
That we came here to find each other again

To smile those smiles again
With new faces
And the same one-track eyes

When the light returns
We finally see

# Song for Badakshan

How can you touch us like that
Then walk away without looking back?

You said you'd never be away
But for thousands of moments we felt alone
And what sustained us?

Your Light, your songs, the dances our fathers taught us
The promise you made to our grandparents
That a new day was coming
The promise that you would return to these vistas
That we would feel your smile and sit at your feet
And be filled with your kindness, your gentle kindness
That we had been praying for
Since we were born

And we feel the weight of much work to be done
And we are ready to take your hand
To follow you to a new tomorrow
A new song for Badakshan

# One Look

It just takes one look to sustain me
One sip of his light, one word
One silent caress fluttering by
As if
By accident

The music plays, and I catch his eye
Dancing together, yet apart
Bodies responding, melding
Despite the gulf between us

Will I feel him when life unfolds?
When our paths don't cross again?
When the autumn comes and leaves drop?
When the icy winds of winter test my love?
When I walk around the fire with someone else?
What will be left of us?
Who are we after we leave each other?

What will it take to sustain me?

# Will You Sleep?

Do not sleep away these tender moments
As eyes and head become heavy
Let another awake-ness Light you.

As the match strikes
Let your own fire spark,
And crack open these old memories.

Use this darkness
To know this new Light
This fresh, ancient Light
That you have carried in dimness
Far too many ages.

We are waiting for you to move aside
So we can see You again.
We know you have been hiding
And today is your time
Your name has been called
Will you stand up and answer
Or will you sleep?

# Yet I Fight

So what will the vision look like?
My eyes flutter closed, sleep overwhelms
Yet I fight
The rhythm of dreams would be so much
Easier
Yet I fight
To live in darkness and complain about
The darkness
Would be so much easier
Yet I fight
The hopelessness surrounds me and
Even tries to enter the heart
This numbness would be so much
Easier
Yet I fight
Fight for the courage to meet his
Eyes and drink his light
When he is ready to grant me them.

# On to the Stage

Who is making these choices?
We steal away for a few flushed moments
Hungry for each other
… Hungry for that burn.

Who makes these choices?
In the middle of the day
 the middle of the night
No food, no sleep, just the breath.

You place your stamp on my soul
 and I learn a new smile for you.
Who makes these choices?

When did we decide that this dance was not dangerous?
A lifetime of
Four days ahead of us,
Four nights
Four stolen glances,
Four secret smiles.
You shake your head at me, I laugh.

Who makes these choices?
My heart pounds in my ears
Ice only makes me hotter.
Every touch, every look pulls me deeper into you.
The room fades and only your brightness pulls me.

Who makes these choices?
Remembering the curve of your neck when I close my eyes,
Tasting it when I get a chance to be close enough.
Waking me from sleep and directing me to your kisses.
Who makes these choices?

You asked me to get out of the audience and join the stage.
So the walls melted and I shone for you,
 and it felt like it's always felt.
Who makes these choices?

There is only one of us here.

# Your Yes

The mountains between us have moved
And I can see you now
And I see an old friend
Who walked with me on many paths
Who I found again to return a favor

That meeting of lips took me back to
The you I knew before
The you I knew when I was not free
And it only took ten thousand journeys
For our paths to cross again

Will you walk beside me
Oh you of the wandering heart?
Will you link your finger with mine
And find the courage to trust me with
Your broken, molten, melted heart?
Will you lay your head in my lap
And pour out the pain?
And let me fill the empty spaces
With the light you shone on me
So long ago?

Give me your yes and I give you
My life
Just like last time

# When He Turned Away

Why has my Beloved turned his eyes away from mine?
He told me my light was too bright
That he was not ready to be ignited yet.
He showed me how quickly I tremble
His electric glance begins my soul beating.

His eyes woke me up again.
He bit his own lip and my lips bled.
His hand on his face warms my skin.

And yet he turns his eyes from mine,
leaving me lightless.
I watch him quenching his thirst,
wishing I was the water that soothed him,
remembering the moments I was the balm
He journeyed for.

But now I am lost
Only his eyes will make me found again.
Perhaps he is afraid that our joining will cause a tremor
The kind that does not remain secret.

Perhaps I do not please his favour.
Perhaps he has found a more lasting union
Beyond the eyes and the heart and the rumblings of
    lifetimes together.

But why has he let go of the gaze?
Why has he turned his eyes from mine?
It was that look that feeds my yearning,

That keeps me anchored
That calms my madness.

And the memory of those eyes is not enough.

Why has he left me so deeply?

# Seeing Him in Concrete

Gentle kisses from the beloved
As rain touches my face
I am even seeing Him in concrete now
In the glimmer of the glass-front buildings
In the heat from the carburetors
Where do we find God when there are no more green spaces?
Cultivating the seeds inside the deepest Me
So my growing may turn my face to Him
As sunflowers in a field
Can't help but look for
Gentle kisses from the Beloved.

# The Change

It's not like I have nothing to say
You just haven't given me the chance

You sing to me
Your poetry
Then don't allow me to dance

I waited for you every night
With words I don't understand
So when the time came
The night was so much more than I planned

You reached inside my deepest need
And took the fears away

You smiled, you smiled, you smiled

And then came the change
The words, long and deep and bringing sleep
Are new now, are new now
Let me find a way to say

You are what I was looking for more
I implore you
Stay and wait with me to free this dark heart

# Prisoner of Light

Getting ready to leave you
Yearning for one more kiss
From your eyes
How quickly we fell together
How deeply I took you into me
And our jail gets tighter
This prison of longing
Suffocating my fear
So that in your eyes
I find my soul-song

# Breathing Each Other

We met under the veil of our night sky
And quickly learned to breathe each other
Fell into a rhythm, into step
Into laughter and song and love
And longing for more time
For one more uninterrupted moment alone

Less than four moments left
Until I never see you again
Never see you like this again

This mehndi smell will have faded
Another man's breath on my neck

But I have found a richness here
That my poor heart never dreamed of

When I felt that drowning, the insanity
I knew what beauty smelled like
And the veils disappeared
I melted into the Beloved

# The Other Side of the River

If only I could hear the words you whisper
From the other side of the river
How I feel your pulse inside me
Tasting the sweet honey nectar
Lips swelling with our karmic poison
Lifetimes of almost yours
The boundaries blur as I drink you
This delicious dizziness pouring into light
The rawness of your hungry mouth
Grazing against my innocence

# Sleep Is Not for Lovers

A sea of faces between us
And still I can see your light
Your tiredness from last night's
Midnight whisperings
Makes me smile
Sleep is not for lovers
Who wake in the darkness
Calling each other's names

# Until

We will keep on asking these difficult questions
Until the inspiration comes

Oh, He who makes me gentle, who makes me drunk
When will You answer these swamp-filled questions?
When will You send me your sweet-water smile?
When will You pour yourself into my skin
And bring me to life again?

Where shall I go to find You when I get lost?
I tried the mosque, the church, the synagogue
I tried dancing, I tried to be still
I tried to swim in the mud and leap off waterfalls

And yet You come to me most unexpected
In the chirp of the morning birds
In the memory of my unborn child
In the long embrace of something that can never be
In the smell of melting chocolate at a summer barbeque

We will keep on asking these difficult questions
Until the inspiration comes
Until the inspiration comes
Until the inspiration comes

Oh, He who makes me ask the questions

# Crying and Cracking

Lovers lie awake, whispering in the grey dawn
Food and sleep an illusion
And the drunkenness is all that is left
Of last night's embrace

He sleeps, and I feel rested
I cry, and his heart cracks open
He smiles, and my cheeks flush
I bring him to the gate, and we are both changed
He moves his arm this way, and my muscles quiver
He moves his arm that way, and I soften
I breathe, and he relaxes

Floating back to when we were one
When walls and lines were golden silk
And there was no space between us

He sleeps, and I feel rested
I cry, and his heart cracks open

Eyelids closed in praise of his name
Saltwater rivers cleansing this promise

He sleeps, and I feel rested
I cry, and his heart cracks open

# A Reason for this Torture

To you who makes me Bruised, Burned,
Destroy me finally
Let blazing stars fall from your Heaven
So I may have a reason for
This torture

So my mind can rest, body becoming water
That flows over you, through you
That pulses through your valley
And towards your mighty ocean
Like the wave's caress on the sand

You wet my heart
Long before you entered my body
And when you did, coming without effort
Evaporating my fear
I knew I had felt this very way before

In a place where there was only
You and Me
Our names spoken together
Or not at all

So destroy me now, take this mind
For there is nothing else I can offer you
Except the promise to find you again
Or wander eternity searching

# The Sweetness

As I try to move away from you
I walk with the urgency of molasses
Keep me stuck in your sticky sweetness
And melt me slowly
Extending this warm agony

Cool breezes may distract my skin
But you wait for me
In the humble space of my own longing

And as long as you wait
I shall continue to return
To the place where you brought me

Back to myself
Back to my God
Back to all the pieces that had
Shattered

Holding me together with your honey
And pouring me into a new Me

# The Tremors

What happened there
In the first hours of the
Morning
When I agreed to join his heart?
Did we lose something?
Did we make an agreement
Stamped by our sails ages ago,
And wake up to the promise?

His face stoic
No clue to the rumblings underneath.

Or maybe there are no rumblings and it's all in me.

This lava moving slowly through
Me
Heating up the desire
As only molten earth can do.

The words will not stop

I thank him for bringing me out of my pier
Into the garden.
I have wanted
To smell these flowers for so long ... to feel the grass
        growing between my
Toes, and all it took was the courage to drown in his eyes.

So here, the shaking begins.

Just a little ripple in the stones of the wall but
Then a tremor, a quiver, a tear falls.

Salty river eyes, lashes dripping with the
Sweet agony.

The longing fills me up to the throat, so I choke back the
    words rushing
Through my mind when his eyes meet mine.

And those eyes both intensify and still
The tremors.

And he melts me.

# Released

This candle burned
Your hot wax melting my
Indecision
And so I surrender
To this gentle eternity
A soft longing for forgotten moments
These invisible bonds that
Tied me to your spirit
Broken
Severed
Released
So we may live again
And feel the beginnings of a smile
When the wind blows the leaves
Just so
Or the clouds creep secretly
To cover the shiny moon

# Kali and Yemoja

It is time for a quick change
A flash of lightning
To clear the mist
A forest fire
To purge the rotting
I ask you to bring the
Thundershowers
The hail
The sleet and snow
For my awakening
Is of a different kind
My light was found at
The bottom of an ocean
And only the blue whale saw
The truth
But now you ask me to
Swim out of these depths
And set fields aflame
To burn in my truth
To walk alone with your name
On my lips
And I submit
And I submit

# After the Suffering

He tells me I am at a crossroads, but I see no choice here.
The path is straight.
And though the steps are not yet clear,
I have already taken the first one.
But ...
Yet ...
I feel empty with these questions.
So I guess if that is all we had then
That one sweet memory would be enough.
When I think of the words we whispered,
I remember a true intoxication.
And now, shy, exposed, I begin to bleed.

Okay, I really want to avoid him now;
Perhaps this is a quick burn
Hot and quick and never materializing.

The journey through suffering
To the love of God
Is not a journey we can talk about
There are no lines between creation and destruction
But suffering will make you reflective
Desire comes first, then the fires of suffering and longing grow

He will only give us as much longing as we can bear

# It Was You

The lights had turned off and the words jammed in my pen
Looking out from behind the walls
So high so deep
I had forgotten that it was you who pulled my forehead to
    the ground
It was you, oh Lion of Allah, who reminded me to pray
    between my prayers

Let me find time to be alone with you
Let us have endless lazy afternoons where I can gaze into
    your eyes
Let me sleep, but lie awake in your love
Let this deep-heat night never end

Love does not make room for sleep

For the eyes of the beloved
Wait for my heart

A blink is too much separation
So how could I spend an hour away
From that gaze?

My body falls, mind falters
And still I seek that nectar
Let me have the courage
To wake

# The Scholar's Curse

He removes the beauty from art
Giving words to the unspeakable
The curve of calligraphy straightened
By his scholar's pen
The colours reduced to mathematics
Instead of the pigment of the sunset

His eyes scan for jet planes
Instead of letting the harmony stir him
He deciphers marks on the paper
Instead of breathing in her perfumed skin

He takes his allergy medication
Droning words with no rhythm
Walking without hearing his inner drum
Studying ballroom dance by watching videos
Not knowing how to let the movement pierce him

How can a man of science not be an artist?
He uncovers the majesty, the mystery, the truth
And yet misses the glimmering
He has quieted his spirit, dimmed his light
Let go of the Believer in him

So now he has a full head
But an empty heart
And does not even feel the yearning of his soul

Until the day that he will be touched
Until the day he will be slapped

Until the day his theories fail him
And all he can do is fall to his knees
And beg mercy
Mercy

They know not what they do
When they remove the beauty from art
And the melody from their hearts

# The Only Release

I want to bleed, to feel the pain on the outside
Cut these wrists and let the velvet redness drip into
The clear, warm water
This is the only release from wanting
The only gentleness would be my body limp
Returning to the quietness I came from, I lived in
Tearing the creamy rose petals
With the edges of my rawness, jagged fingernails
Leaving you as I find myself

# If I Had a Choice

What would I prefer...
His body or his eyes?
Here we sit, nearly touching, heat pouring
Through my skin
And yet I seek his eyes

Hands send me to shivers, his touch raises my skin

But oh those eyes

That melt my barriers
That cause the rivers to rush seaward

The hungry tigress, teeth on bone
His eyes wake up that orange-black wildness
And put to sleep my doubt
Put to sleep my racing mind
Sending insanity into the folders of my mind

He reminds me to remember my smile
Teeth flashing, body poised
And takes me to my freedom

# The Pale Moon

As you fly away to a new life
How will you remember?
Will we be just a dusty memory?
A faded silhouette from a stolen moment?
How will you tell the stories?
And who could you even tell?

Will you remember our dancing?
Will you remember my eyes?
Will you be able to get my scent off your skin?

How will you find me again …
How will we find each other?

You asked me to cry only at your funeral
But this too is a death

The end of a golden moment
That peaked as beautifully as a sunset

And though the moon has a pull
Those mesmerizing glows
The memory of those mesmerizing glances
Will sustain me when I pray

But how will you remember?
Worse,
Will you ever be able to forget?

# Seeing Your Signs

Tell me about Your signs

How the raindrop kisses an autumn leaf
Then falls to the Earth without regret

How Hawk circles above when I feel alone

Tell me about Your volcanoes and earthquakes
That erupt from my belly when I lose Your light

Show me Your brilliance in the greens of the forest
In the pebbles of the river that collect by the banks

This way asks for gentleness, to walking upon Her tenderly
As if holding an infant for the first time

Show me my softness and slow me down
So that the fragrance of Your lilies
Washes my conscience
Unlocking the secrets that I knew once
And I yearn to know again.

# When the Light Fades

The fear creeps into my bones
Everything is ending as the light fades

What holds us together but this thread of a dream?
What binds us but that imprint on my soul?
What makes him find my eyes but the sun he sees in me?
And what to do as this sun begins to set?

Maybe it's the moon that will speak for us now
The mystery and sweetness of the seaside changes
The salty air as ocean crashes over us

Maybe all we need is moonlight
As we have learned to find each other in the darkness

# The Wash

I wondered whether it was brainwashing
Now I see how they washed my brain

The doubts dissolved and the flame ignited
With a truer lover, and a new devotee

Falling in love with my Lord again
With His mind, His eyes, the Light He held

For my mother, my grandmother, those forgotten
For my brothers who know Him not

Hiking to the mountaintops and gathering
The Believers

He has arrived in my heart again
Now that my brain is washed

# The Rebirth

This shaking began last night
In the time between eyes closing and sleep
A tremor as your fingertips grazed my lips

You asking me to speak only truth

My lips obliging
Thirsty for the taste of you

As we dance together, hips rolling
Coming together on the cliffs of madness
And diving off laughing
Ready to crash on the jagged rocks

To be born again
Into a new kind of shaking

# The Lover Leaves

This night, he says farewell
A brush of lips, a smile
A graceful walk away

I try not to follow

But the night drags without him
Sleep does not relieve my racing heart

Leaving me while she searches for him
For she cannot breathe without his
Breath on her neck

For she cannot smile without his grin
For she cannot think without his calm
Turning, turning, she tries to find him
Again

But her looks are too much like the sun
And her lies flow like lava, creating
New vistas
And he walks away, gracefully

Refusing to look back
Refusing to light her up again

# Fears into Butterflies

Who are these soldiers
That do not wear armour or even stand strongly
But move fluidly before their Commander?

Who are these soldiers
That know when to speak
When to listen
When to study
When to demonstrate the message
Through loving their children?

Who are these soldiers
That see the darkness creeping gently
And move aside to let it pass?

Who are these soldiers
That have etched the promise
On the bottoms of the wells and
The peaks of the mountain tops?

Who are these soldiers
That reach across oceans
When someone is pondering a quiet death?

Who are these soldiers
That light the torches with their own stillness
And softly quell the storms with open arms?

Who are these soldiers
That keep coming back

Ready to lift the smiles of the scared ones
And turn fears into butterflies?

Who are these soldiers?

In the name of Allah

Who are these soldiers?
Who are these soldiers?

# Sweet Forgiveness

I saw his light
The glow from the inside
And he became shy

So hard to walk away

And a first lover's quarrel
Falling asleep to his breath on my neck
After sweet forgiveness

But now the distance
He misses me
Yet I know that even when
Our bodies have blended
We won't be close enough
And we will keep coming
Back to each other

To remember our union
That started in a dream

# One More Sip

What gets compromised once the sun comes out?
Is it the cloak of the moon that showed me my Beloved?
Or a trick of the eye …

Did I thirst for it so deeply that my own heart created the oasis?
Or was it real, more real than this body of tissue and bone

That fortress wall reinforced with the first rays on the horizon
And I lost myself, lost myself, lost myself
Lost Him

And through that losing, through that letting go
I find freedom … no, the promise of freedom

And the fierce, sweet thirst for one more sip of His eyes

# Joining

We finally let go, joining at the hips, the lips
The heart
Eyes blazing

The same hands that tilted my chin
Clasping my arms behind my head

The same mouth that uttered that sweetness
Whispering my mind into madness

The same legs that brought you to me
Tangled and quivering with our flame

I finally let go, and so found my foundation
Nothing left of these bones, this sinew

But light, light, light upon light
Pouring my liquid light into you,
I finally let go

The clock melted, the sun rose
Ages passed and I saw the whole stay
Blackness around us, yet I could see your glow

So when I finally let go
I could smell your chocolate
I could taste your fragrance

How everything turned inside out
How my mind stopped and my heart started

How I found the truth
In paradox

In the most unexpected of places

In the curve of your neck
The pads of your fingertips
The drum of your once upon a time

Stirring the ages alive
I finally let go, and gained my life
Felt its grace, its movement, its rhythm
I exhaled myself and inhaled you
And there were no more veils
When we finally let go

# When You Decide To

When Oshun pounds through you
You cannot help but be beautiful.
Even the pouring of water
for a thirsty traveler
becomes an act of worship.

And nothing is ever lost,
just transformed,
like the water that escapes
from the lips
and drips
down the chin.

See how you become my oracle, and I your Teacher?

And when the clouds of doubt enter your mind
and the veils of loneliness separate us in your heart
I promise to remind you of this moment.

And when your vision blurs
and you cease to hear her calling to you
from her mystery,
I will show Her to you in my eyes.

And when your inner voices become
petty and cynical
and forget
that indeed it was Her that brought us
into these bodies,
I will give you my brightest inner-light-smile
so that you remember Her truth.

If you can promise to hold my gaze,
we will both see Her grace.
If you hold my hand as we walk together,
we will find the house of soul food faster.
And if you can let me help you fight your demons,
you will see that indeed, there is no fight.

So let this beauty bring you back to yourself
and breathe Her in through me.
And send me your eyes so I can keep waking up
so Her words will continue.

But then Her voice reminds me:

No one can be ASKED to join this WAY;
They must feel the call themselves.
He must yearn for it,
Be willing to bleed through the thorns for it,
Be willing to have his world destroyed and his mind taken.
And he must keep making this choice.
So do not ask him to join you
Just be ready for him when he comes.

And so I wait for you to say
  "Let me burn."

# Healing the Headache

There is a pounding,
pulsing,
throbbing
beat
that draws me to his light.

Pulled in by my own heat,
I am hypnotized.
A cool healing balm I rub in
to his knotted temples
so his mind may rest while the body relaxes.

More than instinct, I am drawn to a sweetness.
Oh you of the gentle heart, tell me what this pain is about?
Why do you suffer, and how can I
take it away?

Let me bring you to this lake of sweet water
and bathe you slowly,
hands floating like butterflies over your face.

And how you bow your head in
gracefulness and humility and trust.
Knowing we were meant to do this today,
and in this way.

Remembering an unfulfilled promise, the pounding
thickens.

And now how your eyes run from mine,
darting away like a young deer in a spring forest.
And then you receive the salve,
inhaling it deeply into you,
and allow our healing to begin.

Tired of grunting, your words become music and I the dance.
Your music fills me, flowing over and through me,
releasing the dam that held back that tidal wave of yearning.

And so we become a piece of art
You the colors, me the canvas and both the brushstrokes,
And the wild cackle of the mad artist echoes in our hearts.

The cool and pulsing heat of the Taj Mahal
rises through our feet
as the Earth mother rises through my body,
and I dance again for you.

And the mystery reveals itself for a moment
As we burn the veils between us.

# Will You Burn?

His eyes, burning memories of so many lifetimes
I cannot look
I cannot look away
I cannot form words from this burning

And yet we try to speak them
Try to flirt, playing dangerously at the edge of this fire

Rumi says let the fire consume you
Let the fire consume you so you may know your freedom

For this love is only a drop in the ocean of bliss
That you have been looking for
A signpost along the road to the endless orchard
Fruit dripping with sweet, ripe life

Life that pulses
Life that rushes like the raging river

So when you look into his eyes
It's not about Him at all
It is love itself looking back at you
Asking you to be burned

# A Jagged Good-bye

Since we parted paths
I keep retracing the steps

The good-bye was brutal, sudden
Shorter than the time it took
For my eyelids to flutter

And now the light is distant
I can see it, remember its warmth
But my skin still yearns for the heat

I see you everywhere, in everything
In the walk of that boy
The eyes of the shopkeeper
The smell that takes me swiftly
Knocking me out and leaving me spinning

Why didn't I stop you?
Run into your arms and hold on
My life depends on it
And how can I go on?

Those few moments sustaining me
For the remaining hours of my life
Hours that will be peppered with my memories
And a bond of a new kind

They told me true love can never be lost
Just transformed

I pray this transformation passes swiftly
Else I will remain here
In this place of jagged mirror shards

Where once stood the Beloved

# When the Light Leaves You

When the Light leaves you
And your mind settles for blackness
You become inconsolable
The old joys no longer satisfy
Even the simple things become bricks around the neck

When the Light leaves you
You throw yourself to the ground
Face to the dirt
Streaming tears and swollen eyes
Asking why you couldn't have
One more moment of His grace

When the Light leaves you
You realize your fragility
What it means to be bound
To this form
Where you were once the Master of Time
You now become its slave

Hours upon hours of empty grief
Worse than the tears because it suffocates
Looking for anything to drug the mind
And quiet the body

When the Light leaves you
You break all vows
Forgetting what you had promised
The One who made you

You break all vows
Throwing out your joy, the purpose
The drive to know Him
And getting lost, instead, in this place without words

I spoke to Him once in poetry
The words forming a song that moved us
And when He heard me singing
He laughed
He had been waiting for us to recognize His Light
In each other

But we were too busy
Too busy planning and re-planning
Riding to the tops of our ladders
Too busy to remember
That we came here to find each other again
To smile those smiles again
With new faces
And the same haunted eyes
So when the Light returns
We finally see

# Mending the Water Pot

Who are you, anyway
Oh, the boy who broke my water pot?
Who stole my toe rings and anklets
Who smeared my lipstick with your hungry mouth?
Are you the one who chased me
Who laughed under a cornflower sky
As girls in bright colors sang songs for their lovers?

Oh, the boy who broke my water pot
Why didn't you stay?
We promised each other lifetimes
But you left in only moments
The water cascading down my shoulders
And my cheeks
You took my water
You took my smile
You took the secret parts of me that I had been hiding
Wrapped them up in a cloth
And put them in your pocket

Now to get them back, I must journey
But I cannot get to you by air or sea
Even land is too rough to navigate
This reaching you will be of a quiet kind
When a melody stirs me
When my babies laugh
When the sun dips below the horizon just so
That is where I will find the boy
The boy who broke my water pot

# Afternoon in London

Grey cloud, grey cement
Heels crashing on this concrete soil
No one looks at you here
Or a quick glance, then eyes scuttle to something more
Mundane
Less human
Than two brown eyes searching theirs
"Too intimate," they say
Or
"We're in a hurry!"

Do they take a moment when their children need their eyes?
Or their grandmothers?
Do they slow down when the ancestors come to their dreams?

When the Warrior arrived in this green-less place
What did he think of
These tight-lipped, no-song people?

# If I Could Have It My Way

As I wander under cloud-filled skies
My feet burn
Sandals slapping sidewalk
Reminding me of how he walked away

I waited for one last glance, a look back
Peering through the rain
At the back of your head
But that is all I wanted, right?
To know you're happy
In the bed you made

But if I could have it my way ...

We would spend together these
Sweet days and salty nights
Lips burning
Mind still
As we wandered beneath these cloud-filled skies

# His Hipbone

I used to long for their bodies
For the warmth of their chests
For the smell of cologne
Where neck meets shoulder
For their arms around my waist

But something new emerges as I remember him

It's his laughter
The crinkles in the corners of his eyes
The left hand with the band
That ties him to her
His hipbone
The body that I never explored
The spirit that I never left a mark on
That is what I long for

# Freeing the Old Stories

This way to that and this way again
Why do we repeat ourselves?
Telling old stories again and again
Crying old tears

We are ready for a new story
One that ends not with my heart beat
Dying just outside the gate

A story where no one loses
No one suffers
There is no need for tears, old or new
Where, light upon merciful light,
We are shown a new way to be

A rosebush shorn of thorn
Fragrance sweeter and colors popping
The willow tree crying our sadness for us
Breezes swaying her branches
The sunflower turning her face towards her Beloved
Whether or not the skies are veiling Him

This is how we remember the new story
For the signs are plenty
If we remember to look
And free the old stories

# My Sweet Elixir

More than I expected

From our first shy hello
To being able to tell a story without a word

From walking beside you, bubbling with life
To lying beneath you, my sweet elixir

From the brush of a yellow flower
Sunshine on my skin
To nails grasping flesh
The desperation of a secret embrace

From the nervous preparations of body and mind
To breathing each other on the tile floor

From sleeping quickly and waking alive
To loving each other through the night
And bleary-eyed, seeking sleep with dawn

All I need is one hello
Nothing more
Yet so much more
Than I expected

# Serena's Eyes

When you look into her baby brown eyes
Do you see the promises she came to fulfill?

Do you see her growing, changing, wanting to love you
More fiercely than you've ever known love?

Do you see her little body
Trembling with the changes?

Or do you see her gentle soul, still and patient
Waiting for her form
To match the greatness she came here for?

She came here to teach us
And as her wings unfold and her wisdom pours forth
Let us soar with her and remember to remember
Where we came from

Those eyes are not of this world

# Remembering Us

These stolen moments
Whisper as we squeeze in the words
So much to say to you until I hear your
Voice
And then
The smile prevents my lips from moving

There is a bitterness creeping
Along the edges of us
Pray our lights are bright enough
To melt it

Else the world will sweep us away
And all that would be left
Are the stolen moments we had
Soul-gazing
Giving names to the shapes in the clouds

# Turn Me to Steam

Waves of heat as you look across the room
At me
Short of breath

Moisture rises in the hidden spaces
Desire stirring on the back of my neck
To drink the cool sweetness of your touch
The familiar rhythm of your dancing feet

You hold me close
One hand casually pulling me into you
The other in my hair

Your eyes are always open when you kiss me
Daring me to join even deeper
Even fuller
Even forever

Heat waves as I long for your ice
Turn me to steam
Before I melt

# The Veils between Them

How does the burning inspire me?

The dry desert heat slaps her eyes
And her black veils billow in the
Searing sun

He walks ahead
The bearer of water
And she moves beside him, thirsting

Their bodies brush, arm to arm
Electric
She moves away, the current mesmerizing
But now he is infected with her
Desert musk

This mysterious princess
Eyes alive
Luring him to her blackness
He is blessed with his own
Helplessness

He promises to find her again
To follow her
In another time, another space
When she has freedom
And he has honor

He shouts the promise silently
And the words are carried by the wind

He will find those eyes again
And maybe have the pleasure of seeing
Her face

Until then he will wait behind his veils
While she waits behind hers

# The Blinded Moth

Too many good-byes and too few hellos
It seems with him there is never enough time
Even when we had hours
They passed too quickly
Though each lingering look
Has left itself etched in my heart

What will sustain me now, in this purgatory?
Between what was and what can never be?

We shared a moment in the land of what-ifs
Passing through the fields much too quickly
And when I paused to touch a tree
He vanished
Taking with him all I had become
My innocence evaporating in his leaving

And now I am left with not a dance
These legs have not awoken again
The song cannot be coaxed from its
Secret sadness

The blinded moth, wings burned
Crawls in dirt
Heart heavy
Spirit gone

How does one learn to wait lifetimes?
I'm sure I have done this before, yet
It seems like such a cruel twisting of this
Dagger called love

Too many good-byes
Each one making me bite my lip
And turn my eyes away

# Dancing Drummer

Music
Reminds me of how we danced
Watching each other's drums

Bodies moving while so many came between us
The sweat glistening in the low lights
Eyes closed, smiles wide
Showing off for each other
You pretending like I didn't see you

Then the beat drops

And we find ourselves beside each other
Avoiding your eyes, I press against you
The cover of heat and dark
Hiding your hand on my hips
Guiding me deeper, teaching me your
Rhythm
Highs and lows together

A blending of our legs

My heart's pound drowning out the drum
And when the grey sky descends
Thick cloud smoke suffocation
I clear my mind with that night
Your darting glances
Catching my eyes as you watched me
Dance for you

Yours again

# Night Walk

We took a walk together
The green grass our red carpet
The deep star sky our temple roof

You smiled shyly
A smile I had not seen before
A smile reserved for those you let closer

The trees held our secret
As we watched God walk toward us

And suddenly we were in another place
Another time
Another freedom
Where the signs called us

And we made our vow
To come back to each other
And shine brighter than we dared
The last time

# Everything Relaxes

That first encounter

A shy schoolgirl getting dressed for a date
Him watching her movement
Eyes searching for the invitation

Words in a double play
Coaxing her out, testing
They discuss their worst-case scenario

Then everything relaxes

And they fall into step
Like familiar lovers
Who knew each other before they met

And so they begin

Rediscovering what was left behind
Renaming what was never fully formed
Replacing fear with anticipation

And they learn of the freedom to breathe

# Finding Him Again

The water has changed me
As the tree gave me kisses
I knew He knew me
Knows me
And all I have to do
To hear Him again
To feel His kisses
His mercy
His light
Is find the green spaces
Where water flows

# What Sustains Me?

When everybody leaves me, I must turn to the pen
How do I quiet this raging burn inside of me?
As I prepare for a new beginning, so much of me is falling
    away
And there are no rules here

The words flow so effortlessly
My new companions
And no matter how miserable
How empty
Pen to paper takes away the sting

I have been looking outside myself
For something I have always found within me
And I know this

It is time
It is time to go back inside
And cultivate the jewels that are waiting
Yearning to be polished

No one's voice makes me feel the way I did
Today when the trees gave me blessings
Learning to be in this world
While living in a magical place

# My Soldier

I terrorize his mind
Black eyes, drawing him too close
A smile that disarms him

He takes off his shield
The weapons falling from his hands
And he becomes my servant

Wanting only to see the promise of a smile
My voice a torture
My fragrance driving him to insanity

He cannot leave
Yet his honour does not allow him to stay
So he remains, one foot in either world
A mind plagued with unkept promises

A soldier of Love
Killing himself a thousand times
For one glance from the Beloved

# What Is It?

What is it that pulls us toward each other?
Is it that playful pinch, that teasing way?
That look of longing, then eyes avert?

Is it the safety, the warmth, the knowing I will be loved,
  cherished?
Is it the insatiable thirst to devour every piece of me?
Is it the way he respects my mind, is in awe of the way I
  think?
Is it his calm, tender touch when he is trying not to worry
  for me?
Is it his love pouring forth, even though we are in different
  worlds?
Is it the dreams we never realized, lurking in our what-ifs?
Is it the challenge, the fight, the will to win?
Is it the laughter, the belly-aching-on-the-floor laughter
  that makes hours fly?
Is it the innocence we see, the details we notice?
Is it the desire to please each other, to make each other's
  wishes come true?
Is it the generosity, the way he makes me golden?

# The Code

Let's talk about this code
The mathematics of love
The uncrackable, eternal
Brain-frying code
Where you never know if
You've got the right answer
And Plan B is not an option
This code that keeps you up at night
Writing poetry
This code that makes you open your eyes
To watch him kiss you
This code that makes you feel the heat
Even on the prayer mat
My teachers failed me
When it came to Love
Can you teach me the code?

# Preparing the Bride

They shower me with gold
Preparing the bride
Tears spilling onto cheeks
As we said good-bye to our childhoods
A new journey
The path lined with the dreams of our elders
The signposts of wisdom guiding each step
These revived traditions
Songs that shake us in words we don't understand
Colors evoking memories we never knew we had
Smells of a country whose soil we've never seen
Blending into this beautiful moment
As they shower me with gold

# Sweet Torture

This torture goes deep
You dance through my mind when waking
And now you've entered my dreams
When did you
Get under my skin?

Being so far from the Beloved
Is the burning of sand on bare feet
Unbearable, unavoidable
And I have no shoes
As I have been reckless in this love
At least when walking on hot coals
You have a choice

This test is thrust upon the Believer
And nothing can soothe the mind
Quench the thirst
But the arms of the Beloved
Step closer or turn away?
This torture goes deep

# When Others Rise to Pray

Let me get drunk as those with no memory
Of life before you
You came secretly, but once you came
I could not deny you

Now my seeing is blurred
My heart stumbles towards
One more moment of your
Deadly wine
A poison I am told

But when I drink you
My life changes

Let me get drunk on you
Night after night
And when others rise to pray
Let me sway in you instead

# What Melts Me

When I am asked to write for him
The ink freezes
How can I say how everything has changed?

Meeting him was like waking up to my breath again
Kissing him was a thunderbolt, rooting me to him forever
Holding him was like being a child again
His strength, the warmth of his arms

But what melts me are his eyes
Love showering through
And pouring into me

How did I find this hidden gold?
Closer to my heart than the blood that pumps through it

The ink flows

# Praise His Name

Exuberating
That is what he asked her
"What are you exuberating?"

There have been interpretations
Renunciations
Miscommunications
And then he asks
"What are you now jubilating?"

Oh, my king
There is no way to sing
This memory
I have in me
Of time before time
When he was mine
And crisp
Sublime

All one is his direction
Joined in our emancipation
And how we rise again
To make a mark on history
On the path of He
Who knows our way
But will we stay?

Will we be true
To he who
Knows us better than
The jugular vein

And when the rains came
Did we scatter
Or did we stay and flatter
Him
Praise his name
Praise his name
And do not look away.

# My Last Poem

I thought I had written my last poem
I threw down the pen and walked away
From you
But you had made an imprint on my soul

No matter how I struggled to tear you from me
Your smile lit me up
And your face appeared when I closed my eyes
Your gentleness, your sweet care
Followed me into the darkest alleys of my doubt
Shining so that I could see the Truth of us
And kept me believing

I tried to let you go
And you kept coming back
I tried to push you away
But you had already become me
I tried to numb myself, to forget,
To pretend it was all just a passing season

Then I felt your hand on my heart
And realized these bodies are irrelevant
And distance is only in the mind

I brought you into me, let you mix with me,
And now we cannot be separated
For we have colored each other's spirit
You have made an imprint on my soul

CPSIA information can be obtained at www.ICGtesting.com
Printed in the USA
LVOW100123120412

277216LV00001B/2/P